SOCCER

WHO DOES WHAT?

BY RYAN NAGELHOUT

Gareth Stevens
PUBLISHING

Please visit our website, www.garethstevens.com. For a free color catalog of all our high-quality books, call toll free 1-800-542-2595 or fax 1-877-542-2596.

Cataloging-in-Publication Data

Names: Nagelhout, Ryan.
Title: Soccer: who does what? / Ryan Nagelhout.
Description: New York : Gareth Stevens Publishing, 2018. | Series: Sports: what's your position? | Includes index.
Identifiers: ISBN 9781538204139 (pbk.) | ISBN 9781538204153 (library bound) | ISBN 9781538204146 (6 pack)
Subjects: LCSH: Soccer–Juvenile literature.
Classification: LCC GV943.25 N34 2018 | DDC 796.334–dc23

First Edition

Published in 2018 by
Gareth Stevens Publishing
111 East 14th Street, Suite 349
New York, NY 10003

Copyright © 2018 Gareth Stevens Publishing

Designer: Sarah Liddell
Editor: Ryan Nagelhout

Photo credits: Cover, p. 1 bikeriderlondon/Shuttestock.com; jersey texture used throughout Al Sermeno Photography/Shutterstock.com; chalkboard texture used throughout Maridav/Shutterstock.com; p. 5 makieni/Shutterstock.com; p. 6 SOMKKU/Shutterstock.com; p. 7 JiriCastka/Shutterstock.com; p. 9 Mitch Gunn/Shutterstock.com; pp. 11, 17 (soccer field lines) Ammarin Thangsunan/Shutterstock.com; pp. 11, 17 (grass) ANURAK PONGPATIMET/Shutterstock.com; p. 13 Andrey Yurlov/Shutterstock.com; p. 15 The Washington Post/Contributor/The Washington Post/Getty Images; p. 16 daykung/Shutterstock.com; p. 19 Laszlo Szirtesi/Shutterstock.com; p. 21 Gabriel Rossi/STF/Contributor/LatinContent WO/Getty Images; p. 23 Herbert Kratky/Shutterstock.com; p. 24 Jan Kruger/Stringer/Getty Images Sport/Getty Images; p. 25 Kent Horner/Stringer/Getty Images Sport/Getty Images; p. 27 BRG.photography/Shutterstock.com; p. 28 Patsy Michaud/Shutterstock.com; p. 29 Fotopress/Stringer/Bongarts/Getty images.

Printed in the United States of America

CPSIA compliance information: Batch #CS17GS: For further information contact Gareth Stevens, New York, New York at 1-800-542-2595.

CONTENTS

Words in the glossary appear in **bold** type the first time they are used in the text.

LOTS TO KNOW

You might call it soccer, but others call it football. Either way, you're talking about the most popular sport in the world! The object of the game is simple enough—kick a ball into a big net. But if you've ever watched a soccer game, you know it's not that easy.

Soccer is often low scoring because everyone is so good at their job. And there are many different jobs on the field. Each team gets 11 players per team, and every team is different. So let's take a look at soccer from every position—from keeper to striker!

SPIKES AND PADS

All you need is a ball to play soccer, but it's important to play safe. There's some **equipment** that can help you stay safe on a soccer field. Wearing proper shoes, called cleats, can help you keep your footing. And **shin** pads can keep your legs from getting hurt by other players' kicks!

THE KEEPER

The goalkeeper in soccer is special. Not only do they have one of the hardest jobs on the field, they also have a special rule—they can use their hands! Keepers use every part of their bodies to stop a shot on net when they're in the **penalty** area.

Keepers need a lot of different skills. They need to have good **reflexes** to stop shots on target. They must have good hands to catch shots or punch them far away from the net. They must also roll, throw, or kick the ball away to other teammates to start play on offense.

HANDS ON

Goaltenders have another special piece of equipment other players lack: gloves! Gloves help protect fingers from being hurt by hard shots. Keepers learn how to stop shots with these heavy gloves and not give up rebounds, which are when the ball bounces away from the keeper and can be shot into the net again.

THE PENALTY AREA IS ALSO CALLED THE 18-YARD BOX. IT'S THE AREA MARKED IN FRONT OF THE NET.

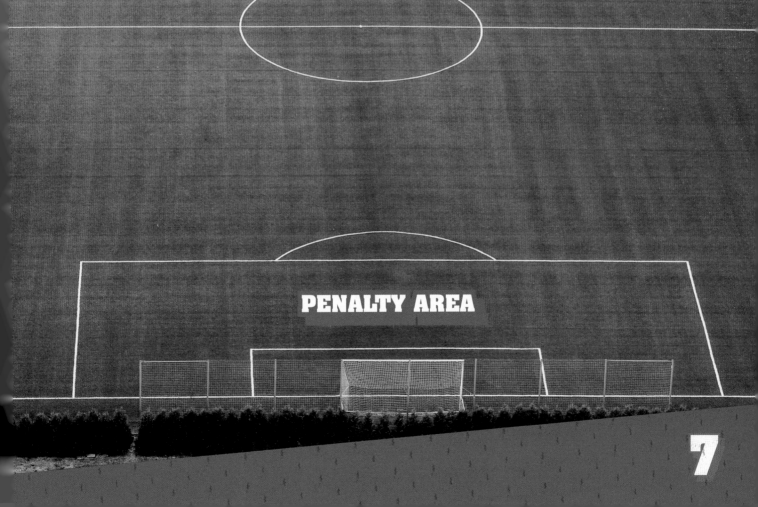

PENALTY AREA

THE BASICS

There are three basic positions played in front of the goalkeeper—forwards, midfielders, and defenders. Forwards mostly play in the offensive zone, trying to score goals on the other team's keeper. They often take passes from the other players on the team and score most of the team's goals.

Defenders mostly play in the defensive zone in front of their goaltender. They make up what's called the back line—the last line of defense trying to stop the other team from getting shots on net. Players can go all over the field, but they have to be careful not to get caught out of position!

BREAKING IT DOWN

Though there are only three basic positions in soccer, each one has a variety of different roles they play on the field. Coaches have to decide how to use their players in different positions and formations that give the team a good balance of offense and defense. Teams need to score goals while stopping the other team from scoring.

GET IN FORMATION

The number of forwards, midfielders, and defenders a team has on the field depends on what formation they play with. A formation is described by how many different kinds of players are used in it, not including the goalkeeper. For example, one of the most common formations in soccer is the 4-4-2. A 4-4-2 has four defenders, four midfielders, and two forwards in front of a goaltender.

A 4-4-2 is considered to be a balanced formation because it offers lots of defensive help to a team's keeper while two forwards try to score goals. Another formation, the 4-3-3, has three forwards to help a team's offensive attack.

A 2-3-5?

Soccer's formations have changed quite a bit over the years. One early formation in the late 1800s was the 2-3-5. That's five forwards with just two defenders on each team! Games had lots of goals because defenses simply didn't have enough players back on defense to stop other teams from scoring!

GETTING IN POSITION

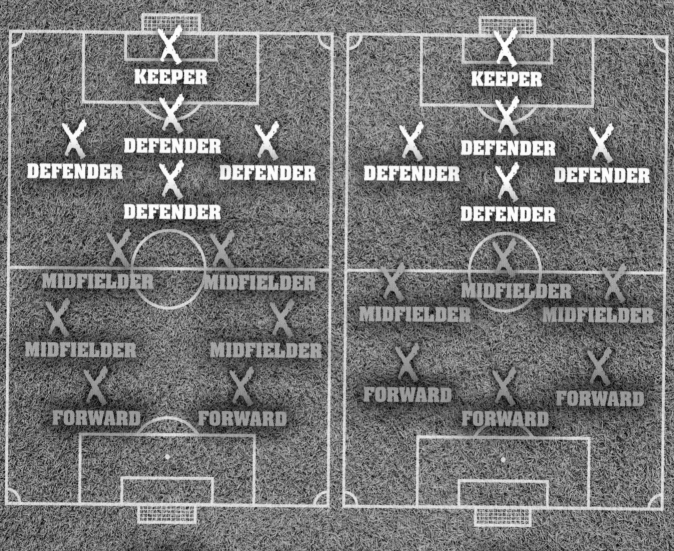

4-4-2

4-3-3

FRONT AND CENTER

Depending on the formation a team uses, a soccer team's defense is made up of many different kinds of defenders. One kind is called the central defender, or center back. In a four-player defense, the center backs are in the middle of the back line.

Center backs need to be strong and good at tackling, or sliding to kick the ball away from an **opponent** without first making contact with the opponent. It also helps if they are taller players, so they can head balls away from the net that the opponent may send into the box.

HALF OR BACK?

Center backs are sometimes called center-halfs because the position was once considered a midfielder. This is a position left over from the 2-3-5 formation where the three midfielders would often stay in the defensive half of the field. Eventually, center-halfs moved to the back line and became the middle of the defense.

FULL UP

Fullbacks lead the way for running backs in American football, but in soccer they play a very different role. Fullbacks play on the outside of a defensive line, guarding the touchlines and helping center backs if the ball is moved toward the middle of the field.

Fullbacks often have to mark, or keep up with, an offensive player called a winger. They need to be smart enough to read what the other offense is trying to do. They also must be fast enough to stop a player on the wing from sending passes to the middle of the field, which are called crosses.

WINGBACKS

A wingback is a fullback that plays a much more offensive role. They play on one side of the field but run deep into the offensive and defensive zones. Wingbacks need to attack like midfielders and forwards but also play defense. They need to be very fast and in good shape to keep up with all that running.

SET THE TRAP

The offside rules in soccer might be tough to understand at first but they're important if you're going to know how to play your position. Offensive players must stay onside, or make sure at least one defensive player is closer than they are to the net when the ball is passed to them. This means players must make a "run" behind the defense after a ball is sent their way.

Back lines often try to "trap" offensive players by moving upfield to put forwards offside. When an offensive player is offside, the **referee** blows the whistle and the ball is given to the other team!

SWEEP IT UP

One defensive role rarely seen today is called the sweeper. It used to play closest to the goaltender behind the other defenders, moving around and sweeping away any loose balls. Today, the term is sometimes used to describe a very active defender or the player with the most skill working on the defensive end.

OFFSIDE RULES ARE USED TO MAKE SURE AN OFFENSIVE PLAYER DOESN'T JUST STAND BEHIND DEFENDERS WAITING FOR THE BALL. IT WOULD BE EASY TO SCORE GOALS WITH JUST THE KEEPER PROTECTING THAT BIG NET!

STAYING ONSIDE

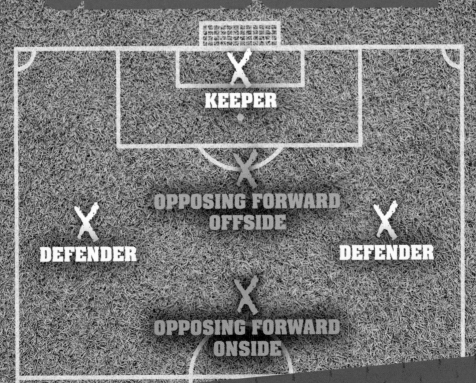

KEEPER

OPPOSING FORWARD
OFFSIDE

DEFENDER

DEFENDER

OPPOSING FORWARD
ONSIDE

MIDDLE OF THE D

A midfield can have up to five players depending on a team's formation. What they're called depends on what role they play on the team. The most defensive-minded midfielders are called defending or holding midfielders. Holding midfielders stay just in front of a defensive back line and try to keep the ball—and opponents—from reaching the back line.

Holding midfielders are good at getting in the way of passes, filling passing lanes in the middle of the field, and putting pressure on their opponent's offensive players. They must also be good at tackling the ball away from offensive players.

CARDS

If a defender tackles a player wrong, they could get a card. There are two kinds of cards: a yellow card, or warning for dangerous play, and a red card that means the player has to leave the game. Two yellow cards in a game are also a red card, and the carded player's team has to play with just 10 players!

IF A DEFENDER MISSES THE BALL ON A TACKLE, THEY COULD GET CARDED. OTHER PLAYS LIKE THIS ARE JUST CALLED FOULS, WITH THE OTHER TEAM TAKING POSSESSION OF THE BALL.

ATTACK FROM THE MIDDLE

An offensive-minded midfielder is called an attacking midfielder. This is often the smartest player on the team. Attacking midfielders are sometimes called playmakers because they're expected to lead the offense. They pass the ball to midfielders and forwards to move it into the opponent's box and get shots on net.

Attacking midfielders need to have good skill with the ball, be able to keep possession in the middle of the field, and feed the ball to others in position to create offense. Attacking midfielders aren't expected to play defense as much as other midfielders, but they can always help out!

BOX-TO-BOX

Central midfielders have a very literal role in soccer. They stay at the center of the field and try to control play. Some central midfielders are called box-to-box midfielders because they run from one penalty box to the other on both offense and defense. They have a lot of skill to control the ball all over the field.

WHETHER A FORWARD OR MIDFIELDER, MANY OF THE BEST PLAYMAKERS IN SOCCER WEAR THE NUMBER 10. THAT'S ONE WAY TO TELL WHO WILL HAVE THE BALL A LOT!

ON THE WINGS

Wide midfielders, also called wingers, play near the touchlines and run up and down the field. These midfielders run the length of the field but often focus on offense, putting pressure on outside defenders and setting up chances for forwards in the box.

Wingers often make plays on offense from the left or right side of the pitch, or field, but they must be able to play in the box as well. The best wingers are great passers that can run fast, setting up quick passing plays that get defenders out of position.

AN ODD POSITION

Wingers are often used in formations that are considered odd because they have an uneven number of midfielders. In formations like a 4-3-3 or 4-5-1, central midfielders worry about the other team's offense while wingers are free to create their own scoring chances, occasionally coming back to help on defense.

UP TOP

Forwards can be seen as lazy by those who don't understand what they do. Often called strikers, they wait for chances to score goals on offense. They often score the most on a team, using their skills to get past defenders and fool keepers with amazing, curling shots.

The striker, or center forward, is the most common. Strikers play closest to an opponent's goal and get the most attention from defenders. They must take passes from teammates and get **accurate** shots past the keeper. Strikers are strong, fast, and able to keep possession of the ball while fighting off multiple defenders.

Soccer balls can dip and curl in the air if they are kicked the right way! One thing forwards must learn is how to kick the ball to make it dip and spin around defenders and past keepers. It's not easy, and sometimes a "strike" will miss badly and sail out of play. It takes a lot of practice!

STRIKERS CAN ALSO HELP CONFUSE DEFENDERS AND MAKE ROOM FOR OTHER SCORING PLAYERS LIKE ATTACKING MIDFIELDERS. TEAMWORK IS IMPORTANT IN SOCCER!

STRIKE HARD

SOME GAMES WILL END IN A SERIES OF PENALTY KICKS IF THE SCORE IS TIED. THIS IS CALLED A PENALTY SHOOTOUT.

TOTAL FOOTBALL

Now that you know the basic positions and formations of soccer, it's time to talk about the styles of play. With teams all over the world, there are many different styles of play in soccer. Some teams like to make lots of different passes.

One style, called "total football," says that every player should be able to fill another's role on the field. If a midfielder moves up with the ball like a forward, for example, another player must take their spot as a midfielder to make sure the team's formation stays in place. It's a tough system to play, but if you're good enough you can play everywhere!

LISTEN UP!

Coaches are often called managers in soccer, but no matter what you call them you better pay attention to them! Coaches can teach you lots of things to make you better at soccer. They can also help you find the perfect position for you on the field.

A COACH HELPS A TEAM FIGURE OUT WHAT KIND OF STYLE THE TEAM SHOULD PLAY. WHETHER YOU'RE PLAYING "TOTAL FOOTBALL" OR SOMETHING ELSE, LISTEN TO WHAT THEY HAVE TO SAY!

GLOSSARY

accurate: free from mistakes; able to hit the target

equipment: the tools needed for a certain purpose

opponent: the person or team you must beat to win a game

penalty: loss or harm caused because of a broken rule

referee: an official who makes sure players follow the rules

reflexes: the ability to react quickly

shin: the front part of the leg below the knee

FOR MORE INFORMATION

BOOKS

Hammelef, Danielle S. *First Source to Soccer: Rules, Equipment, and Key Playing Tips*. North Mankato, MN: Capstone Press, 2018.

Kortemeier, Todd. *Total Soccer*. Minneapolis, MN: SportsZone, 2017.

Laughlin, Kara L. *Soccer*. Mankato, MN: Child's World, 2016.

WEBSITES

Soccer Positions Explained
football-bible.com/soccer-info/soccer-positions-explained.html
Learn more about the positions in soccer here.

Soccer Formations
soccer-training-guide.com/soccer-formations.html
Learn more about popular soccer formations with this illustrated guide.

Soccer Formations and Soccer Tactics
soccer-training-methods.com/soccer-formations.html
Find out more about soccer formations here.

INDEX